The Easy Teenagers' Ultimate Guide to the Stock Market in 2024

A Beginner's Guide to Gaining Knowledge, Confidence, consistency, Financial Freedom and Learning How and When to Invest

Micheal H. Sanchez

Copyright

About the author

Michael H. Sanchez is a seasoned financial advisor with a passion for educating and empowering teenagers to take control of their financial future. With over a decade of experience in the stock market and personal finance, Michael has dedicated his career to demystifying the complexities of investing for young adults. His unique ability to break down complex financial concepts into easy-to-understand language has made him a trusted resource for teenagers seeking to navigate the world of stocks and investments. Through his engaging and relatable approach, Michael has helped countless young people gain the confidence and knowledge they need to make informed financial decisions. "The Easy Teenagers' Ultimate Guide to the Stock Market in 2024" is a testament to his commitment to providing accessible and practical advice for the next generation of investors.

"An investment in knowledge pays the best interest." — Benjamin Franklin

"Bottoms in the investment world don't end with four-year lows; they end with 10- or 15-year lows." — Jim Rogers

"Given a 10% chance of a 100 times payoff, you should take that bet every time." — Jeff Bezos

Table Of Contents

Introduction

How are you doing? Do you feel prepared to take the plunge, or to dive into the realm of early investing? It is in the book that you will learn how putting your money to work at an early age may help you set yourself up for a financially secure future. This book is here to provide you with some fantastic ideas and methods to get the most out of your money, regardless of whether you are just starting in the world of investing or already have some experience in the field.

This book is going to discuss the reasons why it is so great to start investing at a young age, as well as how it may assist you in achieving your long-term financial objectives. We are going to discuss the advantages of beginning your investment career when you are still young, as well as how doing so might potentially provide you with incredible chances.

Get ready to discover all there is to know about the power of investing early on! We will cover everything from the fundamentals of investing to some really useful tips that you can immediately put into practice as you get started. When you have finished reading this book, you will be completely prepared to make intelligent financial decisions and to position yourself for a prosperous future financially. Let's dive right in and find out about the amazing possibilities that are waiting for you to become involved!

The Power of Early Investing

Hey, fellow adolescents! Are you ready to delve into the fascinating world of investment and discover the secret to developing a prosperous future? In this chapter, we're about to go on an amazing tour that will revolutionize the way you think about money and set you up for success.

So, why is early investment so amazing? Well, picture this: you put your money into an investment, and over time, it rises. But here's the mind-blowing thing — not only does your initial investment rise, but the returns on your investment start to produce returns of their own. This snowball effect is called compounding interest, and it's like a magical money-making machine that works best when you start early. We'll show you precisely how significant this can be with some amusing and practical scenarios.

Now, let's chat about the nitty-gritty of investment. We'll lay down the principles of stocks, bonds, and mutual funds in a way that's straightforward to grasp and fully relatable. You'll learn how to make wise judgments when it comes to investing your hard-earned income and appreciate the probable dangers and advantages that come with each alternative.

But wait, there's more! We'll help you identify achievable financial targets and build a bespoke investing plan that aligns with your expectations and ambitions. Whether you're dreaming of exploring the world, founding your own business, or pursuing higher education, we'll show you how early investment may convert your aspirations into reality.

And here's the best part - by the time you finish reading This chapter you'll have the knowledge and abilities to make good financial decisions that will serve you well for years to come. You'll learn how to navigate the stock market like an expert, manage your money with confidence, and take ownership of your financial future.

So, are you ready to harness the immense potential of early investing and put yourself up for a future filled with financial freedom and opportunity? The power is in your hands – let's make it happen!

Why It's Crucial to Start Investing Early

What is the best age to start investing? The great value of interest compounded is the key to begin investing early.

It's crucial to develop financial discipline at an early stage of life to prevent troubles in the future. Early investors have a huge advantage and if you start investing at an early age it may secure a healthy financial future. Teenagers nowadays have the option to start investing at an early stage with the increased accessibility of financial markets and diverse savings tools.

Often, in our early or mid-20s, when we begin our first employment, the appeal of increased financial independence might lead to prioritizing spending above saving or investing. However, learning the skill of managing money is vital for a healthy financial existence. And part of this equation is understanding how to grow and multiply money via investment.

How may investing early be helpful?
Early investments may allow people to build a life they dream of. The magic number for the appropriate age to start investing may not exist, but the answer is clear: start as soon as it is reasonably feasible. The sooner one starts their financial path, the more time their money has to grow and compound.

How much of a difference does it make?
The great value of interest compounded is the key to begin investing early.

Consider two situations: one in which a person begins investing at 25 and the other at 35. The discrepancy in the ultimate amount after 35 years, assuming both invest $5,000 and $7,000 per month, respectively, at a 10 percent yearly compound interest rate, is significant. Early investors would earn a substantial profit of $1.71 million, while later investors would gain $726,500.

What benefits do commencing investing at an early age have?

Early investments create a habit of saving more, leading to better profits in the long term.

Young investors have more time to recover from possible investment losses, lessening the effect on their entire portfolio.

Compounding returns rise dramatically over time, and consistent early contributions may offer large rewards after retirement.

Investing at an early age enhances the prospects of obtaining financial stability in the younger years, offering a feeling of security and independence.

Early investments may operate as safety net amid unanticipated financial problems, delivering a feeling of financial freedom.

Importance of Saving and Investing Early

The benefits of saving and investing early cannot be stressed, particularly for teens who are only beginning to appreciate the value of money. While it may feel like retirement is a faraway notion, the fact is that the sooner you start saving and investing, the more you may profit from the power of compounding.

Imagine this: You're 18 years old, just beginning your first job, and someone urges you to start putting a percentage of your earnings into a savings or investing account. It may not seem like the most thrilling thing to do with your hard-earned money, particularly when there are so many tempting things to spend it on.

However, here's why it's vital to consider:

Firstly, the power of compounding. When you invest money, you get returns not just on your original investment but also on the profits that your investment has already created. Over time, this compounding impact may snowball into a large sum of money. By beginning to save and invest early, you give your money more time to develop, enabling you to possibly build a considerably greater amount by the time you need it.

Secondly, it's about creating solid financial habits. By beginning early, you build an attitude of prioritizing saving and investing, which may set you up for long-term financial success. It's like creating the basis for a robust home — the sooner and stronger the foundation, the more stable and safe the construction will be.

Thirdly, it allows you greater flexibility and independence in the future. Whether it's for further education, purchasing a house, establishing a company, or retiring comfortably, having a strong financial basis may give you with the freedom to pursue your objectives without being hampered by financial anxieties.

Also, it's about taking charge of your future. By saving and investing early, you take control of your financial future. You grow less dependent on others and more empowered to make decisions that match your long-term ambitions.

Although it may not be the most glamorous or instantly gratifying thing to do as a teenager, saving and investing early can make a lot of difference in your financial future. The trick is to start small but start immediately. The advantages of beginning early are not just about money; they're about constructing a secure and rewarding future for yourself. So, take that first step towards financial freedom and see as your money grows together with you!

Basics of Stock Market Investing for Beginners

With investing your funds, the first thing that undoubtedly springs to mind is the stock market, where assets are exchanged. But do you understand what the stock market is or how it works? Do you know what actions to complete or what fees to pay to invest? In this chapter, you'll learn the answers to these and other crucial questions here.

The stock market is where individuals trade fixed and variable income assets, including shares, corporate or government bonds, and exchange-traded funds. A publicly-traded corporation, in quest of funding and capital, sells shares; and investors, who want a return for their money, gain liquidity as the company's shareholders.

A share is a security that offers a shareholder a percentage of a company's earnings. Therefore, shareholders "own" a percentage of the firm in proportion to the number of shares they possess.

To be publicly listed on stock markets, corporations must prove regulators' solvency and transparency, separate from other criteria. The world's biggest stock exchanges by market capitalization are in New York, Tokyo and London.

How much money do you need to invest in a stock exchange?

What is the first step to invest in the stock market?

Before you engage in the stock market, the first thing you must do is get your finances in order. You need to know how much money you make, spend, have saved, and owe to figure out whether you have enough to invest in a stock exchange. Because shares are considered a medium-to-long-term investment, monitoring your finances will also assist you in preparing for the future.

Next, you should comprehend how stock exchanges function. Asking trade specialists, reading financial news, and attending courses are some methods you may receive answers to your queries and grasp essential components of your investor profile, such as your financial objectives, the amount of time you'll need, and your risk tolerance.

Nowadays, applications and websites allow you to open an account to simulate transactions, get more acquainted with the market, and test your investment selections without spending any money.

Once you have gauged your funds and understood your investor profile, the following step is to contact a licensed financial intermediary to execute your trading orders. Because investors cannot trade shares by themselves, two key agencies come into play. The first one is the broker, which may be a person or a firm that is allowed to execute their clients' trading orders for a charge. The second one is the trader, who buys and sells stocks for their gain or that of others.

Traders utilize a broker's platform to make deals.

Which markets and securities should you invest in?

You buy in shares because you anticipate the firm to develop and generate a profit over time. Most experts suggest that you diversify your investing portfolio in terms of businesses, sectors, assets, and geographies so that your money isn't left at the mercy of a single market. You can diversify the shares in your portfolio, but you'll have to make a large investment and do a lot of study.

The stock market communicates not just the status and aspirations of corporations but also the economy as a whole. Environmental catastrophes, political crises, and armed conflict are only a few factors that affect companies' performance and share price.

You may also pick financial goods that are beneficial for the environment and provide you with a return on your investment. Sustainable investment follows environmental, social, and good governance (ESG) principles.

Which financial instrument you should invest in relies mostly on your investment capacity and risk profile (i.e. how much time you are ready to wait for capital rewards). Shares may provide you a return from a company's earnings in the medium-to-long term and can be sold anytime you need liquidity. In contrast, bonds have a predetermined period (usually of five to ten years) for you to recover your investment back together with any capital gains

Three strategies for investing in the stock market:

- Having enough money to invest
- knowing the stock market,
- and picking the finest financial product for your investor profile is, generally, the first step to investing in stock exchanges.

You should also know how to manage your funds depending on your financial objectives.

Getting Started in the Stock Market

Getting started in the stock market may seem to be a difficult task, but it is an essential stage in the process of accumulating money over the long run. Individuals have the option to hold a portion of publicly listed firms and possibly profit from their development via the stock market, which is where shares of publicly traded corporations are purchased and sold. For those who are just starting in the stock market, here is a detailed guide that will assist them understand how to get started.

1. Get Familiar with the Fundamentals It is vital to have a solid understanding of key fundamental ideas before beginning to invest in the stock market. When you purchase shares of a corporation, you join the ranks of shareholders. Stocks are a representation of ownership in a business. Several variables influence the fluctuation of stock values, including the performance of companies, the state of the economy, and the attitude of investors. It is essential to acquire knowledge about the many categories of stocks, such as preferred stocks and common stocks, and how these stocks may be included in your investing plan.

2. To purchase and sell stocks, you will need to create a brokerage account. This is a prerequisite for buying and selling stocks. You may think of a brokerage account as being similar to a bank account; however, rather than keeping cash, it stores your investments. Those who are just starting might take advantage of the many online brokerage platforms that provide user-friendly interfaces and instructional tools. Some prominent examples are Robinhood and TD Ameritrade. When picking a brokerage, examine variables like costs, research tools, and customer service.

3. Research and Select Stocks: Before investing in any stock, it's necessary to undertake extensive research. Look at the company's financial health, competitive position, industry trends, and management

team. Consider aspects like sales growth, profits per share, and debt levels. Additionally, pay attention to external variables that may affect the stock's performance, such as legislative changes or technical breakthroughs. For example, if you're interested in technology firms, you may investigate and consider investing in well-established companies like Apple or growing startups like Zoom Video Communications.

4.   Diversify   Your   Portfolio: Diversification is a crucial aspect of investing. Instead of placing all your money into a single stock, try diversifying your assets among multiple firms and sectors. This helps lessen the danger of big losses if one stock underperforms. You may accomplish diversity by investing in mutual funds or exchange-traded funds

(ETFs), which contain a basket of equities across multiple industries.

5. Monitor Your Investments: Once you've invested in stocks, it's crucial to be educated about your holdings. Keep track of corporate news, quarterly earnings releases, and market developments that may affect your assets. Additionally, frequently examine your investing plan and make modifications as appropriate depending on your financial objectives and risk tolerance.

Getting started in the stock market entails knowing the principles of investing, creating a brokerage account, completing extensive research, diversifying your portfolio, and being updated about your assets. By adopting these steps and learning from your experiences, you may begin your road toward accumulating wealth via stock market investment.

Deciding on What to Invest: Exploring Investment Options

Before you start developing your strategy to become the next Warren Buffett, it's extremely crucial that you grasp the game you're playing and what the odds are.

Picking stocks is a daunting task. There are 11 main stock market sectors, 69 unique industries, more than 8,400 securities, and more than 4,000 listed firms across the major U.S. exchanges. How on earth can anybody – much alone a rookie – go about properly identifying certain equities that are set to perform well?

Right from the beginning, investors should recognize that there's no flawless method or technique that can assure success. As many stocks as there are, there are countless more investment philosophies, plans, tactics, and mindsets that investors employ to approach the market.

As a newbie investor, or even as an experienced market player reexamining your strategy, it's useful to comprehend the following ideas. Here are key factors to consider when selecting stocks:

1. Company basics: Before picking a stock, it's vital to grasp the company's basics. This involves assessing its sales, profitability, debt levels, and competitive position within its industry. Strong fundamentals might signal a healthy and

possibly successful investment opportunity.

2. Industry Trends: Consider the larger industry trends that might affect the company's success. For example, technical breakthroughs, legislative changes, or alterations in customer behavior may dramatically impact a company's prospects.

3. Management Team: Assess the company's management team and their track record. Competent and imaginative leadership is frequently a sign of a company's potential for long-term success.

4. Competitive environment: Analyze the company's competitive environment to learn how it separates itself from its rivals. A great competitive advantage might be a

compelling argument to invest in a specific firm.

5. Financial Health: Evaluate the company's financial health by looking at its balance sheet, cash flow, and profitability. A sound financial foundation may give stability and resilience during economic downturns.

6. price: Consider the stock's price compared to its profits, growth prospects, and industry rivals. A stock may be deemed cheap if its price does not completely represent its growth potential.

7. Dividends and Buybacks: If you're interested in income-generating investments, examine firms that pay dividends or participate in share repurchase schemes. These may offer a

consistent source of passive income for investors.

8. Risk Tolerance: Assess your individual risk tolerance and investing objectives before picking a stock. Some equities may provide bigger potential profits but also come with more volatility and risk.

9. Research Tools: Utilize research tools given by your brokerage or financial websites to gain information about the companies you're investigating. This might contain analyst reports, earnings predictions, and past stock performance.

10. Long-Term view: Finally, approach stock picking with a long-term view. Investing in stocks is about investing in the development of businesses over time,

so examine the long-term potential of the stocks you buy.

The Role of Technology in Stock Market Trading

Technology has transformed the stock market, revolutionizing the way equities are traded. Making investment more accessible and efficient. With the introduction of technology, the market has become speedier, more data-driven, and available to a larger spectrum of investors. In this chapter, we will analyze The Impact of Technology on the Stock Market. Technology has enhanced the speed and precision of stock trading, allowing investors to obtain market information and make educated investment choices.

Technology plays a huge role in the stock market, touching practically every part of the investing process. The following are some important ways that technology is altering the stock

<u>Online Trading Platforms</u>

Technology has made it simpler and more easy for customers to purchase and sell stocks. Online trading platforms enable users to invest in the stock market from their computer or mobile device, removing the requirement for a broker to physically execute deals. This has made investing more accessible and easy for people and has contributed to a rise in the number of individual investors engaging in the stock market.

High-Frequency Trading

Rapid-frequency trading (HFT) is a sort of algorithmic trading that employs complicated algorithms and modern computer systems to execute deals at rapid rates, frequently within milliseconds. This sort of trading has grown more widespread in the stock market thanks to developments in technology. It has a big influence on the way equities are traded. HFT has contributed to improved liquidity in the stock market and has allowed traders to take advantage of market opportunities more rapidly and effectively. Real-Time Market Data Technology has also made it feasible for investors to obtain real-time market data, including stock prices, trading volumes, and news updates. This information is crucial for making educated investment choices and helps investors to respond rapidly to market movements.

Artificial Intelligence

Artificial intelligence (AI) and machine learning are rapidly being applied in the stock market. They examine market patterns, anticipate stock values, and provide trading signals. AI systems can analyze large volumes of data in real time and generate predictions that are difficult for humans to make. AI-powered trading algorithms are growing increasingly sophisticated and are being utilized by hedge funds and other financial entities to gain an advantage in the stock market.

Blockchain

Blockchain technology is a decentralized ledger that records transactions and gives transparency and security to the stock market. This technology offers the ability to simplify the stock trading process, minimize the need for middlemen, and boost the efficiency and security of stock trading.

The Impact of Technology on the Stock Market

Technology has a tremendous influence on the stock market, affecting the way equities are traded. They impact practically every part of the investing process. Some of the significant influences of technology on the stock market include:

- Increased Efficiency

Technology has simplified the stock trading process, making it quicker, more precise, and more efficient. High-frequency trading algorithms, for example, have allowed traders to execute deals in milliseconds, lowering the time it takes to purchase and sell equities.

- Increased Accessibility

Technology has made the stock market more accessible to a larger spectrum of investors. Online trading platforms have made it simpler for consumers to purchase and sell stocks, and real-time market data has provided investors access to the knowledge they need to make smart investment choices.

- Improved Data-Driven Investing

Technology has given investors access to large quantities of data, which they may utilize to make educated investing choices. Artificial intelligence (AI) and machine learning algorithms are widely employed to assess market trends. They produce trading signals, offering investors additional tools to manage the stock market.

- Increased Liquidity

The improved speed and efficiency of stock trading facilitated by technology has contributed to greater liquidity in the stock market. This improved liquidity has made it simpler for investors to purchase and sell equities, which has helped to promote the expansion of the stock market.

- Increased Competition

Technology has made the stock market more competitive, with new competitors entering the market and employing technology to gain an advantage over conventional investing firms.

- New Risks

While technology has given numerous advantages to the stock market, it has also presented new threats. Risks include the danger of cyber attacks and the possibility of algorithmic mistakes. They might have a huge influence on the stock market.

Understanding the Stock Market

You may have watched movies such as The Wolf of Wall Street or The Big Short that make the stock market look like a very chaotic place (particularly with actors like Leonardo DiCaprio or Brad Pitt providing over-the-top Hollywood performances). But these films don't truly educate us a lot about this real-world financial sector.

The stock market is a marketplace where stocks, which are units of ownership in a corporation, are purchased and sold (it's right there in the name!). But what precisely occurs on the market—and how everything works—can appear incomprehensible, particularly in the 21st century, when technology (as opposed to Leo and Brad) plays a large role.

A fundamental grasp of essential ideas, including stocks and shares, markets and exchanges, and the mechanism behind trading, can help you demystify the world of the stock market for youngsters. It may even generate an early interest in saving and investing for adolescents (and goes a long way in explaining some of those Wall Street movies, too!).

What precisely is the stock market?

It's typical to say "stock market" or "stock exchange" as if you're talking about the same thing. But there's one crucial distinction. When you speak about a stock market, you're talking about a set of stock exchanges. Examples of stock exchanges include the Toronto Stock Exchange (TSX) and the Canadian Securities Exchange (CSE). This set of exchanges makes up the marketplace where equities are purchased and traded.

What are stocks?

Buying shares or stocks indicates you're investing money in a firm ("shares" and "stocks" are used to signify the same thing, but shares are the units stocks are measured in, like kilos). When a corporation "goes public," it indicates that it's willing to sell stocks to investors, generally to obtain funds for the firm to expand. As a stockholder or shareholder, you're a part-owner of a corporation. By holding a specific amount of ownership in the company you've invested in, you're now entitled to certain benefits.

Depending on the sort and quantity of stock you acquire, you might be entitled to a percentage of the company's earnings, called dividends, as well as the opportunity to vote on certain corporate decisions at shareholder meetings. Plus, there's the idea of capital appreciation: the difference between the price you acquired the stock at and its current price if it's gone up. If the price goes higher, your stock is worth more. If you decide to sell at this moment, you may earn a profit on that sale.

Types of stocks

Here are the two sorts of stock you're usually likely to hear about:

1.Common stocks

prevalent stocks are—you guessed it—the most prevalent form. They're what we spoke about above a sort of stock where owners are paid dividends, and they get to vote at shareholder meetings.

2. Preferred stocks

Preferred stocks frequently don't enable shareholders to vote, but when it comes time to pay dividends, these shareholders' payments are prioritized above those of regular stockholders. Dividends on preferred shares are normally paid out according to a timetable and at a specified amount. The second distinction between ordinary and preferred stocks is that if a firm goes bankrupt, preferred stockholders are paid out first when the corporation sells its assets.

Because of each of these criteria, preferred stocks are considered a more secure investment than ordinary equities.

How are stock prices determined?

Pay even casual attention to stock market news and you'll undoubtedly note that stock values tend to increase and fall frequently—sometimes simply little, other times drastically. Why does this happen? The answer might be convoluted and include numerous aspects, but there's also a brief list of fundamental principles—namely, supply and demand.

Once equities become accessible on the market, they may be purchased and sold by investors. If a lot of investors are eager to acquire a specific stock, this increased demand might drive the price upward. On the other end of the range, if a lot of investors are seeking to sell a certain stock, the price might plummet. High demand indicates higher stock prices, whereas low demand means lower stock prices.

The "ask" and the "bid" represent the two sides of a negotiation to determine a stock price. The ask is the amount the seller is willing to accept for their stock, while the bid is what the buyer is ready to pay. The price of a stock is decided when the ask and the bid are equal.

What is a stock exchange?

We touched on this previously, when we were going over the distinction between the stock market and stock exchanges. To recap: stock exchanges are like the TSX and others that make up the bigger stock market. A stock exchange is a marketplace where traders and investors buy and sell stocks, as well as bonds and other forms of assets. Canada is home to numerous stock exchanges that make up the Canadian stock market. Here are a handful of the bigger ones:

- Toronto Stock Exchange (TSX)

Canada's biggest exchange is also the third largest in North America—only the New York Stock Exchange and the Nasdaq are larger. The TSX started its origins in 1861 and is currently the site where stock from more than 1,500 corporations is purchased and traded. It's been a purely electronic market since 1997.

- Montreal Exchange (MX)

While the TSX may be Canada's largest market, Montreal is home to the country's oldest exchange. It was formed as an informal forum to purchase and sell railroad and bank stocks in 1832. The exchange made things official in 1874, and in 2007 it was bought by the organisation that runs the TSX. The MX is a derivatives exchange, meaning it offers a sort of financial contract, the value of which is connected to a physical object. That asset might be precious metals, like gold, or cash, like the U.S. dollar.

- Canadian Securities Exchange (CSE) For smaller firms, the venue to issue their shares is on the CSE. Founded in 2003, this electronic exchange includes 770 Canadian businesses that are designated as "micro-cap" or "small-cap" organizations with a total dollar market value that's far smaller than the huge corporations listed on the TSX. The CSE is located in Toronto but also maintains offices in Vancouver.

- TSX Venture Exchange (TSXV)

Calgary is home to the TSXV, an exchange created in 1999, like the CSE, to offer a venue for trading small-cap firm equities. Since it's based in Alberta, it may not surprise you that many firms on the TSXV are resource exploration companies, but IT companies are also prominent on the market. It presently counts 1,649 businesses.

- Nasdaq Canada

Run out of New York City, Nasdaq Canada is the Canadian branch of the Nasdaq exchange (it was formerly located in Montreal). Opened in 2000, the exchange enables for real-time, rapid trading of the more than 5,000 equities listed on the American Nasdaq market. Nasdaq is an abbreviation for National Association of Securities Dealers Automatic Quotation System.

Primary market

A stock is born! Here, on the main market, firms engage with investors to sell an initial offering of shares in their company. This is the entrance point for firms in the quest for finance. Investors are purchasing shares of the firm from the corporation, as opposed to buying from other shareholders. In 2020, organizations like Airbnb and DoorDash both provided the public an option to acquire shares on the main market.

Secondary market

The secondary market is for equities that have been around the block once or twice (or a few hundred times.) This is where investors engage with one another, buying and selling shares that have already entered the stock market via the primary market. These equities are flowing from investor to investor, rather than from the firm to the investor. Examples of these sorts of stocks include Nintendo, Apple, and Amazon—companies that went public decades ago.

What determines stock prices?

Going beyond supply and demand, which we examined before, there are additional variables that impact the price of stocks. These may cause that number to climb or decline, depending on certain economic and industrial conditions:

1. Industry performance

In many circumstances, firms that operate in the same industry are exposed to the same economic causes. For example, if a drought produces a big tomato scarcity, then it's reasonable that the whole ketchup sector would be impacted by the decline in tomato availability. Typically, this would imply the price of ketchup would climb, as would the price of ketchup business shares.

2. Company news

Imagine the same ketchup firm announces that it's recently signed a contract to sell ketchup to a huge burger chain. Again, demand for ketchup has gone up, although this time it's not for the whole industry, but for a single ketchup producer. Both positive and negative corporate news, however, may affect stock values. A ketchup controversy or recall might potentially bring down stock values.

3. Bear market

The way investors feel might also impact stock prices. When investor confidence in the market is low, stock prices might decline. This is termed a bear market.

4. Bull market

The opposite of a bear market is a bull market, when investor confidence in the market is strong, and stock values tend to move up.

5. Economic or political shocks

Do you know that one friend or family member that detests surprises? The stock market is like, "Same!" When something significant and unexpected occurs on a global or national level, it might impact the stock market's stability. Examples of these types of occurrences might include the shutting of a national border, disputed election results, or a natural catastrophe that prevents access to supplies.

The History and Evolution of the Stock Market

Stock-like instruments may be traced back to Ancient Rome, when people acquired shares in public businesses active in different sectors, such as construction and shipbuilding.

The notion of stocks further evolved in medieval Europe with the establishment of joint-stock organisations, allowing people to engage in voyages and commercial enterprises. Merchants and dealers established different structures for investing including the selling of shares and partnerships.

The first stock exchange: 1602

The first recognised stock exchange was the Amsterdam Stock Exchange founded in 1602. Initially, only shares for the Dutch East India business could be exchanged, making it the world's first public business. Eventually, additional firms were added and the exchange offered crucial features including listing fees and regular trading hours. This would all build the framework for future stock markets.

New York Stock Exchange formed: 1792

The first version of the New York Stock Exchange was created in 1792 with the signing of the Buttonwood Tree Agreement. This agreement structured securities trading among 24 separate brokers on Wall Street. The daily gathering to buy and sell assets would ultimately evolve into the New York Stock Market (NYSE), currently the biggest stock market in the world.

London Stock Exchange formed: 1801

When the Royal trade was initially built in 1571 to enable the trade of commerce and precious items, stockbrokers were not permitted within the building. Instead, these individuals enabled securities deals at the neighboring Jonathon's Coffee House because of their boisterous and belligerent character. Stockbrokers were not authorized to do business at the Royal Exchange until it was rebuilt in 1669 after being burned by the Great Fire of London. In 1773, a more official trade was founded in Sweeting's Alley. This became the official site of the London Stock Exchange by 1801.

Hong Kong Stock Exchange formed: 1891

The Hong Kong Stock Exchange was initially created as the Association of Stockbrokers in Hong Kong. It would not become known as the Hong Kong Stock Exchange until 1914. Since then, it's become one of the biggest in the world as the city has also risen in significance as a major maritime port and commercial hub.

Wall Street Crash of 1929

While other market panics happened in the first century of major markets' existence, the collapse of 1929 was the greatest to date and is usually recognized as the first comprehensive market crash.

A stock market crash is a quick and unexpected decline in prices that impacts not just a few firms or sectors, but the whole economic market. The crisis of 1929 happened after a decade of unprecedented economic growth, which raised prices to unsustainable heights. It was one of the key reasons for the Great Depression that lasted until 1941.

NASDAQ formed: 1971

Headquartered in New York City, the NASDAQ is the most active exchange in the United States and the second biggest in the world by market capitalization. It was also the first electronic exchange.

The advent of electronic trading on the NASDAQ drastically lowered bid-ask spreads, quickly making it a contender against big exchanges like the NYSE and driving other exchanges to adopt electronic too.

Black Monday: 1987

Black Monday was another dramatic market crisis that saw major US stock indexes lose up to 20% of their value. Many economists consider Black Monday as a price correction after a highly inflated market, akin to the collapse of 1929 succeeding the roaring twenties.

Other variables, such as a triple witching the Friday before and global fear leading to a bank run, led what may have merely been a market correction to spin out of hand.

Shanghai Stock Exchange formed: 1990
Stock trading started in mainland China as early as the 1860s, and numerous sorts of stock exchanges were formed in the following decades. However, all stock markets were shuttered in 1949 once the People's Republic of China came into control. Stocks and bonds weren't traded again until the 1980s, and the modern Shanghai Stock Exchange launched in December of 1990.

Euronext stock exchange formed: 2000
Euronext was founded as a combination of the Amsterdam Stock Exchange, Brussels

Stock Exchange, and Paris Bourse. It was developed to take advantage of the unified European currency. It is presently the fourth-largest stock exchange by market value after the NYSE, NASDAQ, and China's Shanghai Exchange.

Euronext operates in various European Union member nations, making it a very complicated and highly-traded market.

Dot-com bubble: 1999 - 2000

The dot-com bubble erupted when a fast spike in new technology investments failed to achieve the amount of profit anticipated by the new enterprises. The emphasis on internet-based enterprises in the collapse is where the term derives from.

Financial crisis: 2008

The financial crisis was another significant stock market meltdown after a phenomenal bull market that spurred speculative investors to manufacture subprime mortgages — high-risk loans given to potential homebuyers that led to huge defaults by the borrowers. The real estate market had overextended these loans and eventually crashed when borrowers were unable to pay them back.

Coronavirus crash: 2020

The fast spread of the coronavirus essentially shut down industry and substantially affected global commerce. Selloffs grew so severe that many markets quickly ceased trade after plummeting more than 10% in a single day.

The Impact of the Global Economy on the Stock Market

Global events may have a major influence on the stock market. Changes in the economy, foreign relations, political conditions, and other outside variables may impact the pricing of shares and the overall performance of the market.

Many individuals regard the stock market as a roller coaster ride with shifting pricing. However, investors frequently forget that other influences, particularly international events, may impact how well equities go. It's crucial to notice that everything in our world is interrelated. So, it is necessary to think about how global events might impact the stock market.

Economic Crises

If an international incident causes an economic downturn in one or more nations, it may send ripples across the global economy and stock markets. Investors may become more risk-averse, leading stock values to decline.

One of these turning moments occurred in 2008 when the global economy was heavily damaged by the financial crisis. The financial crisis originated on Wall Street when a group of mortgage-backed securities broke apart because they were backed by faulty subprime mortgages. While this was a financial event, the ramifications stretched beyond the financial markets. Many individuals in the United States became homeless, and there was a bailout by the U.S. government. Additionally, the Canadian, European,

Asian, and other foreign markets felt the repercussions to some degree, even though they had no role in the actions going place on Wall Street.

Geopolitical Events

Political events with worldwide consequences, such as Brexit or geopolitical crises, may affect the stock market. For example, the Brexit vote in 2016 produced volatility in financial markets as investors faced the uncertainties surrounding the UK's separation from the European Union.

Trade Disputes

Trade conflicts between large economies may produce market instability. Tariffs, retaliatory measures, and concerns regarding trade policy may impact firms' profitability and investor mood, leading to swings in stock prices.

Natural Disasters

Hurricanes, earthquakes, and floods are all instances of natural calamities that may affect corporate operations, supply networks, and customer demand. This may lead the stock market to be erratic.

Health Crises

Pandemics and other health emergencies may dramatically influence the stock market. These things may make it hard for firms to function, create issues in the supply chain, and make individuals less interested in purchasing something. For example, COVID-19 became ubiquitous in early 2020 and rapidly influenced the stock market. Global lockdowns shut down companies and prompted many individuals to lose their employment. This generated issues in the supply chain and the economy, which damaged the global financial markets.

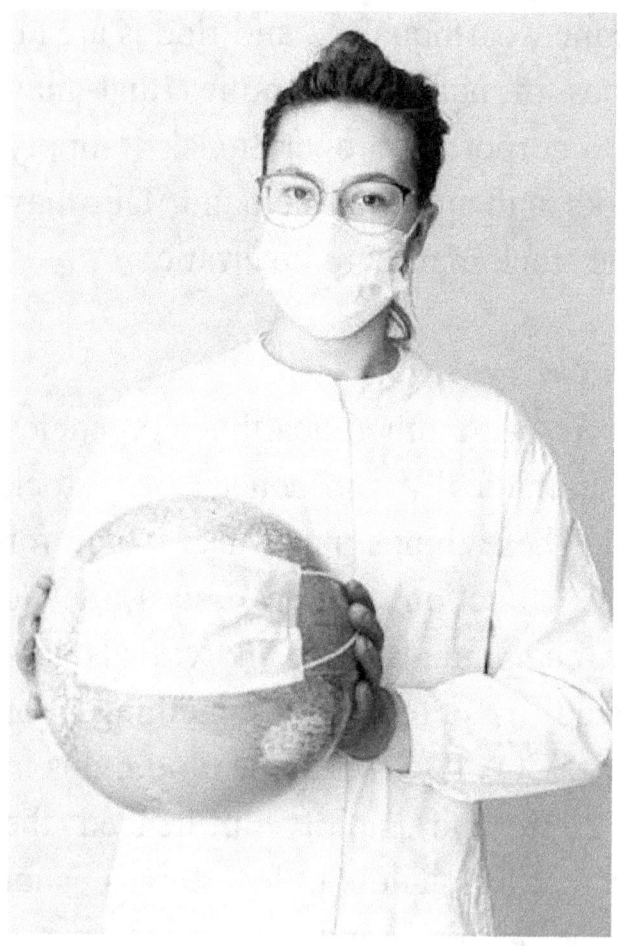

Changes in currency exchange rates

Currency exchange rate fluctuations may affect international commerce, which can affect how much money a firm produces and how much its stocks are worth. International events may also generate swings in currency exchange rates, which can influence the profitability of firms that do business in numerous countries and lead to a decrease in stock values.

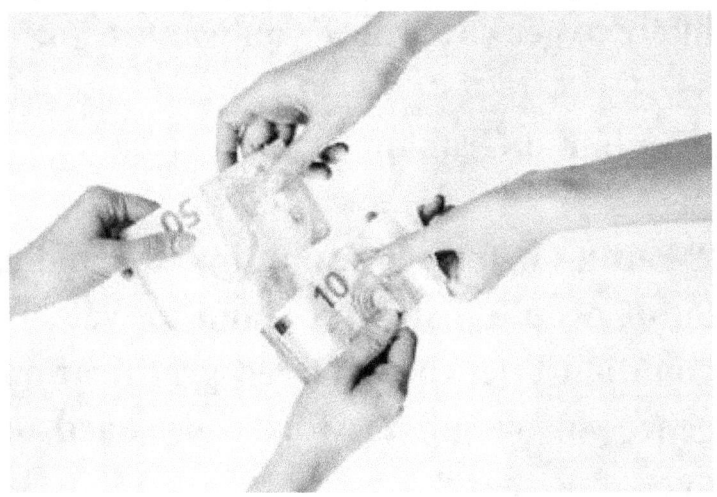

"Invest for the long haul. Don't get too greedy and don't get too scared."

_Shelby M.C. Davis

"The best way to measure your investing success is not by whether you're beating the market but by whether you've put in place a financial plan and a behavioral discipline that are likely to get you where you want to go."

_Benjamin Graham

"Waiting helps you as an investor and a lot of people just can't stand to wait. If you didn't get the deferred-gratification gene, you've got to work very hard to overcome that."

_Charlie Munger

Strategies for Successful Investing

Strategies for Investing may be a vital strategy for generating wealth and accomplishing financial objectives. However, for newcomers, understanding the intricate world of investing may be frightening. Understanding the techniques for successful investment is vital for making educated choices and optimising profits. Here's a complete summary of crucial tactics to assist newbies start on their financial journey:

1. Establish Clear Financial objectives: Before plunging into the realm of investing, it's vital to establish clear financial objectives. Whether it's saving for retirement, purchasing a house, or paying a child's education, having precise goals can drive your financial selections. Determine your investing time horizon and risk tolerance depending on your financial objectives.

2. Educate Yourself: Take the time to educate yourself on alternative investing choices, asset classes, and investment vehicles. Understand the fundamental ideas of stocks, bonds, mutual funds, exchange-traded funds (ETFs), real estate, and other financial products. Additionally,

educate yourself with fundamental financial ideas like as diversification, risk management, and the power of compounding.

3. Diversify Your Portfolio: Diversification is a basic approach that entails spreading your assets across numerous asset classes and securities. By diversifying, you might possibly minimise the total risk of your portfolio. Consider spreading your investments between stocks, bonds, real estate, and other assets to establish a balanced and robust portfolio.

4. Start with Low-Cost Index Funds: For novices, low-cost index funds might be an ideal starting point. These funds monitor a certain market index (such as the S&P 500) and give wide exposure to a diverse

selection of equities. Index funds often have lower expense ratios compared to actively managed funds, making them a cost-effective option to obtain exposure to the stock market.

5. Practice Dollar-Cost Averaging: Dollar-cost averaging entails investing a certain amount of money at regular periods, regardless of market circumstances. This method may help lessen the effect of market volatility by enabling you to acquire more shares when prices are low and fewer shares when prices are high. Over time, this rigorous strategy might possibly cut the average cost of your assets.

6. Stay updated and Avoid Emotional Decisions: Keep yourself updated on market trends, economic data, and

company-specific news that might effect your investments. However, avoid making hasty judgements based on short-term market changes or emotional responses to market volatility. Focus on long-term investing goals and avoid attempting to time the market.

7. Rebalance Your Portfolio: Regularly examine your investment portfolio to ensure it is aligned with your financial objectives and risk tolerance. Rebalancing includes altering the proportion of your investments by selling overperforming assets and purchasing underperforming ones to preserve your desired asset mix.

Stock Market Investment Strategies for Long-Term Success

There are a lot of various methods to approach stock investing, but virtually all of them come under one of three fundamental styles: value investing, growth investing, or index investing. These stock investment techniques reflect the attitude of an investor and the approach they apply to invest is determined by a variety of elements, such as the individual's financial status, investing objectives, and risk tolerance.

Below, we're going to examine the three fundamental types of stock investment techniques that investors often utilize to approach investing in stocks.

Value Investing Basics

The technique of value investing, in basic words, is purchasing stocks of firms that the marketplace has undervalued. The idea is not to invest in no-name firms that haven't been recognized for their potential – that falls more in the domain of speculative or penny stock investment. worth investors often purchase into solid firms that are selling at cheap prices that an investor feels don't represent the company's actual worth. Value investing is all about finding the greatest price, akin to getting a fantastic discount on a designer item.

When we say that a stock is undervalued, we imply that an examination of its financial statements suggests that the price the stock is trading at is lower than it should be, based on the company's inherent worth. This may be suggested by factors such as a low price-to-book ratio (a financial statistic preferred by value investors) and a high dividend yield, which indicates the amount of dividends a firm pays out each year compared to the price of each share.

The marketplace is not always right in its assessments and hence equities often just sell for less than their real value, at least for some time. If you adopt a value investing approach, the idea is to search out these inexpensive companies and snap them up at a favorable price.

Value Investing Long-Term

The value investing technique is very easy, but executing this method is more complicated than you may think, particularly when you're utilizing it as a long-term plan. It's crucial to resist the temptation to attempt to earn rapid cash based on flighty market movements. A value investing approach is built on purchasing into strong firms that will retain their performance and that will ultimately have their inherent worth recognized by the marketplace.

Warren Buffet, one of the finest and most successful value investors of the century, famously observed, "In the short term, the market is a popularity contest. In the long run, the market is a weighing machine." Buffet focuses his stock picks on the genuine potential and stability of a firm, looking at the entirety of each company instead of merely looking at a cheap price tag that the market has given individual shares of the company's stock. However, he does still like to acquire equities he considers as "on-sale".

The Basics of Growth Stock Investment Strategies

For decades, growth investment has been seen as the yin to value investing's yang. While growth investing is, in the most basic sense, the so-called "opposite" of value investing, many value investors also adopt a growth investing strategy when deciding on companies. Growth investment is extremely similar, in the long-term, to value stock investing techniques. If you're investing in stocks based on the underlying worth of a business and its potential to develop in the future, you're utilising a growth investing approach.

Growth investors are differentiated from purely value investors by their concentration on young firms that have proven their potential for considerable, above-average growth. Growth investors look at organizations that have regularly shown signals of growth and considerable or quick gains in company and profit.

The main premise underlying growth investing is that the rise in profits or revenue a firm creates will subsequently be mirrored by an increase in share prices. Differing from value investors, growth investors may often buy stocks priced at or higher than a company's current intrinsic worth, based on the belief that a continued high growth rate will eventually boost the company's intrinsic value to a substantially higher level, well above the current share price of the stock.

Favorite financial indicators utilized by growth investors include earnings per share (EPS), profit margin, and return on equity (ROE).

A Fusion of Value and Growth

In actuality, if you're contemplating a long-term strategy for investing, a combination of value and growth investment, as Buffet so skillfully does, may be worth your attention. There are significant grounds to back up adopting these stock trading techniques.

Historically speaking, value stocks are generally the stocks of corporations in cyclical sectors, which are primarily made up of businesses providing products and services that consumers spend their discretionary money on. The airline sector is an excellent example; consumers travel more when the economic cycle is on an ascent and fly less when it swings downward because they have more and less discretionary cash, respectively. Because of seasonality, value stocks often do well in the market during periods of economic recovery and prosperity, but they are likely to lag behind when a bull market is maintained for a long length of time.

Growth equities often perform better when interest rates decrease and companies' profits take off. They are also generally the equities that continue to advance even in the late stages of a long-term bull market. On the other side, they are frequently the first equities to take a hammering when the economy slows down.

A fusion of growth and value investing allows you the possibility to experience larger returns on your investment while minimizing a considerable percentage of your risk. Theoretically, if you employ both a value investing strategy for buying some stocks while using a growth investing strategy for buying other stocks, you can generate optimal earnings during virtually any economic cycle, and any fluctuations in returns will be more likely to balance out in your favor over time.

Passive Index Investing

Index investing is a far more passive method of investment when compared to that of either value or growth investing. Consequently, it entails significantly less labor and thinking on the part of the investor. Index investing diversifies an investor's money broadly across several kinds of shares, trying to mimic the same returns as the general stock market. One of the key advantages of index investing is that several studies have shown that few ways of choosing individual companies beat index investing over the long run.

An index investing approach is commonly followed by investing in mutual funds or exchange-traded funds that are meant to replicate the performance of a major stock index such as the S&P 500 or the FTSE 100.

NB: S&P (Standard & Poor's is an American financial intelligence firm that works as a component of S&P Global. S&P is a global leader in the supply of financial market analysis, notably in the development of benchmark and investable indices and credit ratings for businesses and nations.)

Note: An Exchange-Traded vehicle (ETF) is an investment vehicle that holds assets such as stocks, commodities, bonds, or foreign currency. An ETF is traded like a stock throughout the trading day at varying values. They commonly follow indexes, such as the Nasdaq, the S&P 500, the Dow Jones, and the Russell 2000.

Investors in these funds do not directly own the underlying investments, but instead, have an indirect claim and are entitled to a part of the earnings and residual value in case of fund liquidation. Their ownership shares or interests may be freely acquired and sold on the secondary market.

The Role of the Federal Reserve in the Stock Market

The stock market is a complex and dynamic system impacted by several variables, including the operations of central banks such as the Federal Reserve. For novices and teens trying to comprehend the function of the Federal Reserve in the stock market, it's crucial to grasp the fundamentals of how this organization affects stock prices and general market conditions.

1. Monetary Policy: The Federal Reserve, frequently referred to as the Fed, plays a critical role in setting the country's monetary policy. One of the key methods the Fed employs to impact the economy is via the control of interest rates. When the

Fed rises or decreases interest rates, it may have a major influence on borrowing costs for companies and individuals, which in turn impacts spending, investment, and economic growth.

2. Interest Rates and Stock Prices: Changes in interest rates established by the Federal Reserve may directly impact stock prices. When the Fed reduces interest rates, borrowing becomes cheaper, making it more enticing for firms to invest in growth and innovation. This may lead to greater company earnings and higher stock prices. Conversely, when the Fed raises interest rates, borrowing becomes more costly, possibly lowering corporate profitability and causing stock values to decrease.

3. Economic Indicators and Market Expectations: The Federal Reserve regularly analyses numerous economic indicators such as unemployment rates, inflation, and GDP growth. By examining these data, the Fed analyses the health of the economy and makes choices on monetary policy. Additionally, the market constantly observes the Fed's remarks and actions, as investors seek to predict future changes in interest rates and adapt their investment strategy appropriately.

4. Quantitative Easing and Market Liquidity: During times of economic difficulty, the Federal Reserve may employ unorthodox monetary policies such as quantitative easing. This entails the Fed buying huge amounts of government bonds and other assets to pump liquidity into financial markets. This approach tries to decrease long-term interest rates and boost lending and investment, which may have a favorable influence on stock values.

5. Market Stability and Investor Confidence: The Federal Reserve also serves a crucial role in preserving overall market stability and investor confidence. Through its regulatory monitoring and crisis management activities, the Fed tries to avoid systemic risks and financial instability that might severely influence stock markets and the wider economy.

Understanding the function of the Federal Reserve in the stock market is a crucial element of being a smart investor. By keeping a watch on the Fed's policies and their possible effect on interest rates, market players may get insights into how monetary choices may affect stock prices and investment possibilities.

NB: liquidity refers to the ease with which an investor may purchase or sell an asset without materially impacting its price. Essentially, it is a measure of how fast and effectively an asset may be turned into cash without producing a noticeable change in its market value.

How to Analyze and Pick Profitable Stock Investments

Sure! Investing in stocks may be a terrific way to increase your money over time, but it's crucial to learn how to assess and identify lucrative stock purchases. Let's break it down into several basic steps:

1. Understand the business: When you're thinking about investing in a stock, it's crucial to understand the business behind it. Look at what the firm does, how it produces money, and its competitive position in the market. For example, if you're contemplating about investing in a technological business like Apple, you may want to look at how its goods are selling and how it compares to its rivals like Samsung or Microsoft.

2. Check the Financial condition: You'll also want to check at the company's financial condition. This involves looking at factors like its income (how much money company produces), its profitability (how much money it retains after costs), and its debt (how much money it owes). You may obtain this information in the company's financial

statements, which are normally published on their website or via financial news sources.

3. Analyze the Stock Price: Next, you'll want to look at the stock price. This is where some math comes in! One approach to accomplish this is by looking at the price-to-earnings (P/E) ratio. This is a simple formula: P/E ratio = Stock Price / Earnings per Share. The P/E ratio informs you how much investors are ready to pay for each dollar of the company's profits. A lower P/E ratio can imply that a company is cheap, while a greater P/E ratio might signal it's overpriced.

4. analyse Market Trends: It's also crucial to analyse what's occurring in the market right now. For example, during the COVID-19 epidemic, several travel and

hospitality businesses took a blow since people were staying home and not traveling. On the other side, technology and e-commerce stocks enjoyed a rise as more consumers were purchasing online. Understanding these tendencies will help you make more educated investing choices.

5. Diversify Your assets: Lastly, it's a good idea to diversify your assets. This implies spreading your money among various kinds of equities and other assets, such bonds or real estate. Diversification may help lower your risk if one investment doesn't perform well.

Exploring Opportunities in the Stock Market

Investing in the stock market has become more accessible and popular than ever, owing to the spread of Internet trading platforms and the democratization of knowledge and financial resources. In this article, we will discuss the options and techniques for investing in the stock market, with an emphasis on developing a diverse investment portfolio that may give long-term gains and help guarantee your financial future.

Investing is critical for developing wealth and accomplishing financial objectives, especially in an age of low interest rates and inflation. However, investing always entails risk, and it is vital to grasp the foundations of stock market investing and the many kinds of investment instruments available to improve your portfolio and limit your risks.

When a firm goes public and issues stocks, it allows investors to acquire a percentage of its ownership, and these stocks are exchanged on the stock market, where the prices vary depending on several variables, including the performance of the underlying companies, market trends, and economic circumstances. The stock market functions via stock exchanges, where buyers and sellers may trade equities through brokerage companies or Internet trading platforms. Each stock has its price, which is determined by supply and demand.

Stock market trading entails risk and reward, and investors must comprehend the trade-off between the possible rewards and the hazards involved. Long-term investment entails keeping stocks for a lengthy time, with the goal that the general trend will be upward, while short-term investing involves purchasing and selling stocks for a small period to take advantage of market trends and microeconomics.

The Pros and Cons of Different Types of Stock Market Investments

Investing in stocks may be an exciting endeavor; nevertheless, it is essential to have an understanding of the benefits and drawbacks associated with the various sorts of stock market investing. However, purchasing individual stocks comes with a greater level of risk, but it also has the potential to provide big gains. However, exchange-traded funds (ETFs) may incur management costs, even though they provide diversity. The costs associated with mutual funds may be greater, but they do provide expert management. Young investors may benefit from knowledge of these possibilities, which can help them make more educated selections.

1. Common Stocks

In the context of an organization, common stocks are the sort of shares that confer ownership rights on the individuals who possess them. The shareholders of common stock can vote on a variety of issues, including the election of the chairman, the election of the board of directors, policies, and other concerns. Common stockholders have a claim to the assets of the business if the company is liquidated. This entitlement continues even after the firm's creditors, lenders, and preference shareholders have been paid off.

Advantages

- The performance

When compared to government bonds and certificates of deposit, the performance of common stocks is superior. However, there is no maximum limit on the investor's profits from their common stock ownership. Therefore, common stocks are less costly and more practical options versus debt investing.

- Voting rights

One voting right is vested to an investor per share of each common stock owned. These voting rights empower investors to take part in company decisions and the formation of corporate policy.

In certain circumstances, investors have the right to elect the board of directors by exercising their voting rights. The more common stocks investor possesses the more influence they will sway the policies of a corporation.

- Liquidity

Due to their liquidity properties, common stocks may be quickly relinquished or invested by investors. Thus, these stocks enable investors to acquire shares and walk away with all their cash if the firm does not produce outcomes to their expectations.

Liquidity allows the investor's liberty to do with their money what they see fit without any bother.

- Limited Legal Liabilities

Beyond the financial investment events that place inside the corporation, the duties of common shareholders remain, and they need to be concerned with all legal liabilities.

When the corporation is generating rising returns over time, ordinary shareholders know passive beneficiaries of a fixed income of sorts.

Passive shareholders are not accountable in case the firm liquidates or falls into legal difficulty.

Disadvantages

- Market Risks

The biggest risk linked with the common share is the market risk. Market risk is the problem of the firm underperforming over a period.

A major fall in the company's performance might lead to the profit being devoured by the shareholders and not obtaining the dividends they are waiting for.

This is a key feature to examine since ordinary shareholders are not the only and the first ones to enjoy payment advantages even when the firm is functioning incredibly well.

- Uncertainty

Even while common ownership might be considered a fixed-income option, there is no assurance of dividends. However, the significant distinction here is that the income is not guaranteed when one anticipates it dependent on the fund's availability in the organization and how they are spending those funds.

When the corporation begins to disperse dividend distributions, investors and ordinary shareholders are not the only ones to get instant dividends.

They get their dividends after shareholders and bondholders are eligible to collect full dividends. Hence there a degree of unpredictability and lack of control when it comes to the profitability of ordinary stocks.

2.Preference Stocks

Just like ordinary stocks, preference shareholders have voting rights and rights over the assets in the case of liquidation. However, the distinction between common shareholders and preferred stockholders is that the preferred stockholders have a preference or precedence over common stockholders. In the case of liquidation, the preference shareholders will be paid out first, and subsequently common stockholders will have a right to acquire the assets. Similarly, the preferred investors get paid a predetermined dividend when the corporation distributes its excess.

<u>Advantages</u>

- Current Income

Preferred stocks are a hybrid form of instrument that has qualities of both ordinary stocks and bonds. One benefit of preferred stocks is their propensity to pay bigger and more frequent dividends than the same company's ordinary shares. Preferred stock often comes with a set dividend. The corporation is not compelled to pay the dividend and is not regarded in default if it misses a preferred dividend payment as it would be if it missed a bond payment. The corporation is required to pay any missed preferred dividend payments before it makes any dividend payment on its ordinary shares.

- Ownership

Both bonds and preferred stocks are considered fixed-income products since the amount of recurring interest or dividend payments is a predictable feature. The market price of both bonds and preferred stocks is highly impacted by variations in prevailing interest rates. Unlike bonds, which are debt instruments and don't impart any ownership in the firm, preferred stocks are equity products. Preferred shareholders own a portion of the firm. If the firm succeeds well, the value of the preferred stock may rise regardless of interest rate swings.

- Preferential Treatment

In a worst-case situation, a corporation could be obliged to liquidate its assets to pay its creditors. The company's bondholders have the first claim to the company's assets, before the preferred shareholders. Once the bondholders have been paid whole, the company's assets are accessible to the company's preferred shareholders. Any assets remaining after the preferred investors are paid are distributed among the common stockholders.

Disadvantages

Preferred stock often does not contain the opportunity to vote at the company's annual shareholders' meeting. The market price of preferred stock is interest-rate sensitive and may decline substantially during times of rapidly increasing interest rates. Since the board of directors might choose to discontinue dividend payments, no certainty preferred stock will keep its regular supply of current income.

3.Hybrid Stocks

Hybrid stocks are also known as convertible preference stocks. As the name indicates, such kinds of stocks have an option to be convertible into a common stock on a specific date for a predetermined convert ratio. For example, a ratio of 3:2 preference to common equities would indicate for every 3 preferred stocks owned the shareholder would get 2 common shares. Such shareholders may or may not have voting rights

Advantages

Returns from hybrid stocks: A hybrid mutual fund provides active risk control via asset allocation. They lower risk by mixing assets that aren't connected, like stocks and bonds.

<u>Disadvantages</u>

Market risk: Market risk is the chance of a financial setback coming from variations in the stock market's value. This might lead to a large loss of capital if prices decrease too much.

Credit Risk: The fund might invest in financial securities with a negative credit rating, having elevated possibilities of default. This may result in both interest and principal being lost.

Making Money through Stock Market Investments

- Earning from capital appreciation

By investing in shares, one might expect to benefit from capital appreciation, i.e., the gains gained on the capital (principal invested) as the share price rises. The gains or the earnings from shares might reach as high as 100 percent or more. There is, however, no assurance of capital appreciation. The possibility of the market prices staying lower than the purchase price always exists.

- Earning from dividends

A corporation distributes earnings to its shareholders by issuing partial or full dividends. In most situations, the corporation partly distributes earnings and maintains the balance for other objectives, such as growth. The dividends are given per share. "If a firm chooses to offer $10 per share, and if the face value of the share is $10, it is termed a 100 percent dividend."

The formula for determining dividend yield

Dividend Yield = Cash Dividend per share / Market Price per share * 100.

Here is how you may use the formula:

"If a firm chooses to offer $10 per share, and if the face value of the share is $10, it is termed a 100 percent dividend. Say if the market price of a stock is $120 and the dividend announced is $4 per share, the dividend yield is 3.33 percent."

By investing in shares, the danger of losing a substantial portion of one's cash occurs, unless one utilizes a hedging technique.

- Factors affecting stock price

To gain money from direct equity, one has to recognize the elements driving the share price. A company's share price does not fluctuate independently. Several internal and external variables are responsible for it. When a firm is predicted to expand quickly, more individuals desire to hold the shares. This leads to more demand for the stock on the market, which results in higher pricing. Further, acquisition intentions, repurchase offers, announcement of bonuses, and splitting of shares affect prices in the near run.

In addition, there are macroeconomic variables such as GDP, inflation, and interest rates affecting performance and consequently stock prices. If the economy is functioning well, the demand for products and services will be stronger, resulting in increased profits for corporations. Further, high inflation implies higher costs and customers will be able to purchase fewer products and services, harming the company's sales and profits.

- Number crunching

Stock selection needs an understanding of a large variety of areas such as economics, finance, and corporate law. However, if you lack intensive knowledge of these topics you may employ some fundamental ideas. Firstly, you should comprehend the company's operation; and study the company's financial documents including income statement, balance sheet, and cash flows. Don't only concentrate on profits. Balance sheets and cash flows are considerably more crucial.

After you have assessed the company's financial condition, look at its value. solid balance sheet data paired with cheaper values relative to rivals or the index gives a solid argument to purchase. You may utilize many sources to get information about stocks. The first one is the website of the exchange where the stock is listed. Here, you may discover financial reports and corporate news. Companies also post their financials on their websites.

- Building a diverse portfolio

Start by investing your money in multiple equities, which is also called diversification. This diversification should happen across industries and also across stock market capitalizations. Concentrating on one sector or placing all your cash in one market cap may not be the smartest thing to do.

Diversifying across sectors or industries helps if the economic climate is not beneficial for any one sector since each area has its own unique set of elements that affect the success of organizations. These include the economic climate, the cyclical nature of the company, and government policies. By diversifying, one is essentially establishing a stock portfolio, the total return of which matters and not return from any 1-2 stocks out of it.

- Don't attempt to time the market

Knowing the bottom or the top in a stock's history always comes to be recognized in retrospect. Rather than attempting to timing the market, concentrate on the time spent in the market. Waiting for the stock price to decrease farther down may not even arrive and many investors are left out in the waiting game. It's advisable to stagger one's investment at various price levels.

- Avoid herd mentality

When the stock price soars up, many investors feel left out. At times, without knowing the business and the firm financials, new investors hop on as herd mentality takes hold. Such a move might be financially detrimental since it may amount to pure speculation and most investors could be at the mercy of huge operators.

Further, when stock prices collapse substantially in a space of a few days, there might be unresolved issues and anxiety causes contributing to its fall. The price reversal might be similarly quick. Avoid the temptation to make judgments based on gossip or speculative claims.

- When to sell

At times, stock markets might stay flat for a lengthy period, but at other times it can be quite turbulent. Your choice to leave should ideally not be dependent on short-term market fluctuations but on your stock selection. If there are no fundamental changes in your stocks, including its financials and operations, stick to it. possibility is inevitable when investing in stocks and so, one should be prepared to bear the possibility of watching the share price drop down drastically. Keep some chunk of cash in hand to benefit from market possibilities. If your stock has done well, recording gains may not be a terrible idea.

"Far more money has been lost by investors trying to anticipate corrections, than lost in the corrections themselves."

_Peter Lynch

"The idea that a bell rings to signal when to get into or out of the stock market is simply not credible. After nearly fifty years in this business, I don't know anybody who has done it successfully and consistently. I don't even know anybody who knows anybody who has."

_Jack Bogle

"Though tempting, trying to time the market is a loser's game. $10,000 continuously invested in the market over the past 20 years grew to more than $48,000. If you missed just the best 30 days, your investment was reduced to $9,900.1"

_Christopher Davis

Navigating Pitfalls and Common Mistakes

Investing may be a rewarding adventure, giving a road to financial development and stability. However, the path to successful investment is littered with dangers that may derail even the most well-intentioned people. In this chapter, we'll review the 20 most frequent investing errors and give suggestions on how to prevent them.

1. Lack of Research:

One of the cardinal faults of investing is plunging in without extensive investigation. Whether it's stocks, bonds, or real estate, knowing the market, the asset, and its possible hazards is vital. Informed judgements are the core of successful investment.

2. Ignoring Diversification:

Putting all your eggs in one basket is a typical error. Diversifying your investing portfolio among numerous assets helps disperse risk and minimises the effect of a poor-performing investment on your total wealth.

3. Emotional Decision-Making:

Emotions have no role in investing. Fear and greed may distort judgement, leading to rash actions. It's crucial to adhere to a well-thought-out plan rather than responding impulsively to market changes.

4. Chasing Performance:
Investors frequently make the mistake of pursuing last year's winners. Past performance is not indicative of future outcomes. It's vital to concentrate on the fundamentals of an investment rather than following trends.

5. Market Timing: Attempting to time the market regularly is a dangerous venture. Even seasoned investors find it tough to forecast market fluctuations precisely. Instead, maintain a long-term view and remain involved through market swings.

6. Neglecting Risk Tolerance:

Every investor has a different risk tolerance. Ignoring your risk tolerance might lead to difficult circumstances during market downturns. Assess your risk appetite and create a portfolio that corresponds with it.

7. Overlooking Fees and Expenses:

Fees and expenditures may cut into your earnings dramatically over time. Be cautious about knowing the expenses connected with your investments, including management fees, transaction costs, and other charges.

8. Not Having a Clear Investment Plan:

Investing without a clear strategy is equivalent to setting sail without a destination. Define your investing objectives, time horizon, and risk tolerance. A well-defined strategy acts as your financial compass.

9. Herd Mentality:

Following the crowd might be hazardous. Just because everyone is investing in a specific asset doesn't imply it's the perfect pick for you. Conduct your research and make judgements depending on your financial goals.

10. Lack of Patience:

Successful investment needs patience. Markets go through ups and downs, and it's crucial to remain dedicated to your long-term objectives without succumbing to the seduction of rapid rewards.

11. Failing to Rebalance:

Market swings might lead your asset allocation to differ from your original strategy. Regularly rebalance your portfolio to ensure it corresponds with your risk tolerance and investing goals.

12. Not Staying Informed:

The financial scene is changing, and being educated is vital. Neglecting to keep up with market trends, economic statistics, and industry news might leave you ill-prepared to make intelligent investing choices.

13. Investing Without an Emergency Fund:

Before going into the world of investing, ensure you have a healthy emergency fund. This fund functions as a financial safety net, saving you from having to sell assets amid unforeseen costs.

14. Lack of Consistency:

Consistency is crucial to successful investment. Regularly contributing to your investing accounts, regardless of market circumstances, helps you to take advantage of dollar-cost averaging and harness the power of compounding over time.

15. Underestimating Taxes:

Tax consequences might dramatically effect your investment results. Understand the tax consequences of your assets and discover techniques to maximise your tax efficiency.

16. Being Overconfident:

Overconfidence may lead to unsafe choices. Acknowledge that investing contains uncertainty and be modest in your approach. Regularly examine your portfolio and change your approach as appropriate.

17. Neglecting the Power of Compounding:

The sooner you start investing, the more you may profit from the power of compounding. Don't underestimate the influence of time on your investment results.

18. Failing to Have an Exit Strategy:

Knowing when to sell is as crucial as knowing when to acquire. Define clear exit strategy for your investments to lock in profits and minimise possible losses.

19. Investing Without an Understanding:
Investing in sophisticated financial products without a clear knowledge is a formula for catastrophe. If you don't grasp an investment, seek expert guidance or examine alternate possibilities.

20. Not Reviewing and Adapting:
Markets change, and so should your investing approach. Regularly analyse your portfolio, reassess your objectives, and be prepared to adjust to changing market circumstances.

"History provides a crucial insight regarding market crises: they are inevitable, painful and ultimately surmountable."

_Shelby M.C. Davis

"A 10% decline in the market is fairly common—it happens about once a year. Investors who realize this are less likely to sell in a panic, and more likely to remain invested, benefitting from the wealth building power of stocks."

_Christopher Davis

"In the short run, the market is a voting machine. In the long run, it is a weighing machine."

_Benjamin Graham

Looking to the Future

1. It is anticipated that the economy of the United States would enter a period of recession. As a result, the economy will slow down, and therefore, individuals may have less money available for spending. There is a body known as The Conference Board that makes use of several pieces of information in order to forecast when the economy could undergo a shift. The most recent report that they have produced

indicates that the signals are pointing towards a slowdown. The fact that this has occurred so seldom in the past makes it a significant event.

2. We anticipate that a bear market will emerge in the stock market in the year 2024. Even though the economy and the stock market are not directly related, it is common for businesses to see a decrease in earnings whenever the economy has a slowdown. When looking at the past, we can see that almost two-thirds of the occasions that the S&P 500 (an indicator of the stock market) saw a significant decrease since the beginning of the Great Depression in 1929, it occurred after a recession was formally proclaimed, rather than having occurred before. This implies that if a recession hits, it's probable that stock values will also go down.

For the sake of simplicity, let's imagine that there is a business that deals in toys. Because more individuals have the financial means to purchase toys while the economy is doing well, the firm generates a significant amount of profit. The toy manufacturer may sell fewer toys and earn a smaller profit if the economy continues to slow down and individuals have less money to spend than they can spend. As a consequence, the value of the company's shares might go down.

Now, let's take an example using numbers. Imagine you acquired a stake in a corporation for $100. If the economy slips into a recession and the firm begins producing less money, the value of your share can decrease to $80. This is what might happen in a bear market - when stock values decline by 20% or more from their previous highs. So, it's crucial to keep a watch on economic data and news about the economy to comprehend how it can affect the stock market.

3. The yield curve, which depicts the interest rates on various government bonds, has been doing something strange. For the previous 428 days, the interest rate on short-term bonds has been higher than the interest rate on long-term bonds. This is termed an "inverted" yield curve.

Historically, when the yield curve inverts, it frequently suggests that the economy would slow down and the stock market might tumble. Every time this has occurred since World War II, a recession has followed.

Right now, we're in one of the longest inverted yield curves ever recorded. It's as if you could collect more interest from a 3-month savings account than from a 10-year investment. This is unique and implies that investors are apprehensive about the future.

However, analysts say this peculiar circumstance won't persist much longer. They anticipate the government to cut interest rates, which might help the yield curve go back to normal. This might happen by the end of the year.

In plain words, an inverted yield curve is a hint that something could go wrong with the economy, but it's not assured. And there are methods that the government can attempt to remedy it.

4. One business that is not well-liked on Wall Street is anticipated to fare well if the Treasury yield curve inversion resolves in 2024. This industry is mortgage real estate investment trusts (REITs), which might gain from the move.

Companies like Annaly Capital Management and AGNC Investment generate money by borrowing at low short-term interest rates and utilizing that money to acquire higher-yielding long-term assets, including mortgage-backed securities. The wider the gap between the money they generate from their investments and the cost of borrowing (known as "net interest margin"), the more money these corporations may make.

The yield-curve inversion has made it harder for mortgage REITs to make money, but if this situation changes and the Federal Reserve continues its policy of keeping interest rates low, companies like Annaly Capital Management and AGNC Investment could become very attractive to people looking for income.

5. Core inflation" refers to the overall rise in prices of goods and services, excluding the expenses of food and energy. If core inflation continues high or accelerates up, it suggests items will grow more costly over time.

When the Federal Reserve (the central bank of the United States) announces that it wants to decrease interest rates three times in 2024, that's excellent news for many investors. Lower interest rates might make it cheaper for firms to borrow money. This may lead to more people being recruited by corporations, more businesses being purchased, and more new ideas being generated.

But there's a disadvantage. In the past, the Fed has decreased interest rates when the economy was slowing down. However, in the third quarter of 2024, the U.S. economy increased quite swiftly by 5.2%. Now, if the Fed follows forward with its plan to cut interest rates, it may accelerate the pace at which prices are going up (inflation).

The core inflation rate might be extremely high in 2024. For example, let's imagine the core inflation rate is at 3% per year. If it continues high or grows, it might make goods like housing more costly. This might make it tougher for individuals to purchase houses and for the economy to expand at a stable rate.

To reduce the core inflation rate down to the Fed's long-term objective of 2%, the economy may need to slow down considerably. This would imply that firms are not developing as rapidly, and individuals could have a difficult time getting work.

Although lower interest rates may be helpful for some sections of the economy, they could also contribute to rising inflation and make it harder for individuals to finance items like houses.

6. It is anticipated that the excitement around artificial intelligence (AI) will soon go off. The fast expansion of the stock market in 2023 may be mostly

attributed to artificial intelligence (AI). Making use of software and systems to carry out activities that are traditionally carried out by humans is what it entails. AI is expected to contribute approximately sixteen trillion dollars to the global economy by the year 2030, according to experts at PwC.

On the other hand, if we are to believe the past, artificial intelligence could not be a guaranteed success in the near run. Many new investing trends that have emerged over the previous three decades have gone through a period of heightened enthusiasm. Some of these trends later proved extremely successful, while others, such as the internet, business-to-business trade, genomics, 3D printing, marijuana, blockchain technology, and the metaverse, were originally overhyped and did not realize their full potential. Some of these trends eventually became very successful.

7. Over the next year, it is anticipated that Microsoft will make its way past Apple to become the most valuable publicly listed firm. Over the last decade, Apple has maintained its position as the most valuable publicly listed business in the world in terms of market value. The firm's success may be attributed to the innovative products and services it offers. The total growth of Apple, on the other hand, has slowed down, and the company's sales of its tangible items continued to decline in 2023.

On the other hand, Microsoft is on course to grab the top place. Its cloud computing provider, Microsoft Azure, took approximately 25% of worldwide investment in cloud infrastructure in the third quarter. Additionally, Microsoft continues to produce considerable money from its conventional activities like Windows and Office, and it has been making smart acquisitions. All these considerations imply that Microsoft has the potential to become the most valuable public business in the world in 2024.

To grasp this better, let's explore an example. Imagine Apple and Microsoft are like two pupils in a class. For many years, Apple has been the best student, always doing brilliantly and obtaining top scores. However, lately, Apple's ratings have begun to drop. On the other hand, Microsoft has been working hard and increasing its performance, and it's currently on pace to become the top student in the class.

In quantitative words, if we compare the growth rates of Apple and Microsoft, we can see that although Apple's growth has slowed down, Microsoft's growth is rising. This makes investors assume that Microsoft will soon become the most valuable publicly listed corporation.

8. It has been anticipated that Tesla, the world's biggest electric vehicle (EV) company, will see its stock price plummet below $100 per share in the next year. To give you some perspective, by the end of 2023, Tesla's shares were trading at roughly $253.

One explanation for this probable decline in stock price is Tesla's pricing approach. The business has been consistently cutting pricing on its Model 3, S, X, and Y cars into 2023. This shows that demand for Tesla's vehicles is diminishing, inventory levels are rising, and competition in the EV industry is intensifying. As a consequence, Tesla's formerly remarkable profit margins are now more in line with the norm for the car sector.

Another element to consider is Elon Musk, Tesla's CEO. While he is recognized for his forward-thinking ideas, he frequently promises more than the firm can deliver in terms of new developments. Despite being considered as a leader in both the energy and car sectors, Tesla generates most of its money from selling and leasing EVs, which traditionally have lower profit margins. Additionally, a major amount of Tesla's income comes from sources that may not be sustainable in the long run.

In plain English, these variables imply that Tesla's stock price may decrease below $100 per share in the future.

9. Utilities, which refer to corporations that supply critical services like electricity, water, and gas, are anticipated to be one of the top three performing sectors in the stock market in 2024. In 2023, utilities had a terrible year owing to investors opting to invest in Treasury bonds instead, as the Federal Reserve hiked interest rates. This led the performance of utility stocks to decline.

However, in 2024, the central bank is forecast to cut interest rates, which makes utilities more appealing to investors again. One of the reasons why investors enjoy utility stocks is because they tend to have reduced volatility and pay large dividends.

As Treasury bond rates decrease, the dividend yields of utilities become more tempting. Additionally, with access to reduced financing rates, utility businesses may participate in acquisitions and big projects that might enhance their growth rates.

One significant firm in the utility industry is NextEra Energy, which is projected to gain from these possible advancements. For newcomers, it's crucial to realize that utilities are a sector in the stock market that contains firms providing critical services, and their performance may be impacted by things like interest rates and dividend yields.

10. A short-lived crisis refers to a scenario that doesn't persist for a long

period. In this context, it suggests that there will be an issue or trouble that will occur but won't have a permanent influence. It has been forecasted that there will be an unanticipated catastrophe that will momentarily damage Wall Street, which is a prominent financial market in the United States.

Every year, there is generally an unforeseen incident that generates a lot of trouble for the Dow, S&P 500, and Nasdaq Composite. For example, in 2023, there was a crisis in the regional banking sector that didn't continue for a long time but had a big influence on the global financial system. The bankruptcy of three significant banks sparked fears among investors about the soundness of other institutions.

In 2022, Russia's invasion of Ukraine was the key event that generated a lot of unrest. The invasion had political and diplomatic ramifications, which resulted in a short drop in the stock market.

As for 2024, it's impossible to anticipate what type of crises may arise shortly. However, there is a warning that there may be a fall in property values or a wave of defaults on vehicle loans.

Conclusion

I hope that this book has given you a sound basis for understanding the stock market and investing. Remember that learning about the stock market is a constant process, and there is always more to study and discover.

As you continue your adventure into the world of investing, I urge you to be interested, keep learning, and never be hesitant to ask questions. The stock market provides unlimited prospects for development and financial success, and by remaining educated and proactive, you may position yourself for a profitable future.

Embrace the pleasure of researching new investing options and continue to increase your understanding of the stock market. By doing so, you may open doors to financial independence and establish a secure future for yourself. Keep exploring, keep learning, and most importantly, keep investing in your future.

WAGMI

NOTES